1995

Schools in
the Middle

The Practicing Administrator's Leadership Series
Jerry J. Herman and Janice L. Herman, Editors

ROADMAPS
TO SUCCESS

Other Titles in This Series Include:

The Path to School Leadership: A Portable Mentor
Lee G. Bolman and Terrence E. Deal

Holistic Quality: Managing, Restructuring, and Empowering Schools
Jerry J. Herman

Selecting, Managing, and Marketing Technologies
Jamieson A. McKenzie

Individuals With Disabilities: Implementing the Newest Laws
Patricia F. First and Joan L. Curcio

Violence in the Schools: How to Proactively Prevent and Defuse It
Joan L. Curcio and Patricia F. First

Women in Administration: Facilitators for Change
L. Nan Restine

Power Learning in the Classroom
Jamieson A. McKenzie

Computers: Literacy and Learning
A Primer for Administrators
George E. Marsh II

Restructuring Schools: Doing It Right
Mike M. Milstein

Reporting Child Abuse:
A Guide to Mandatory Requirements for School Personnel
Karen L. Michaelis

Handbook on Gangs in Schools:
Strategies to Reduce Gang-Related Activities
Shirley R. Lal, Dhyan Lal, and Charles M. Achilles

Conflict Resolution: Building Bridges
Neil H. Katz and John W. Lawyer

Resolving Conflict Successfully: Needed Knowledge and Skills
Neil H. Katz and John W. Lawyer

Preventing and Managing Conflict in Schools
Neil H. Katz and John W. Lawyer

Secrets of Highly Effective Meetings
Maria M. Shelton and Laurie K. Bauer

(see back cover for additional titles)

Schools in the Middle

Developing a Middle-Level Orientation

Jack A. McKay

CORWIN PRESS, INC.
A Sage Publications Company
Thousand Oaks, California

For information address:

 Corwin Press, Inc.
A Sage Publications Company
2455 Teller Road
Thousand Oaks, California 91320

SAGE Publications Ltd.
6 Bonhill Street
London EC2A 4PU
United Kingdom

SAGE Publications India Pvt. Ltd.
M-32 Market
Greater Kailash I
New Delhi 110 048 India

Printed in the United States of America

Library of Congress Cataloging-in-Publication Data

McKay, Jack A.
    Schools in the middle : developing a middle-level orientation /
Jack A. McKay.
        p.   cm. — (Roadmaps to success)
    Includes bibliographical references.
    ISBN 0-8039-6232-0 (pbk.)
    1. Middle Schools—United States. 2. Middle schools—United
States—Administration. I. Title. II. Series.
LB1623.5.M35   1995
373.2'36'0973—dc20   95-1463

This book is printed on acid-free paper.

95 96 97 98 99 10 9 8 7 6 5 4 3 2 1

Corwin Press Production Editor: S. Marlene Head

Contents

Foreword

Schools in the Middle: Developing a Middle-Level Orientation stresses the process aspects of transitioning as they relate to the specific requirements for creating and maintaining a middle school.

The author presents a comprehensive scope that includes (a) strategies for transitioning from a junior high to a middle school, (b) the history of the middle school movement, (c) research on middle school reforms, (d) leadership skills required to successfully implement a middle school, (e) information related to monitoring progress in a middle school, and (f) methods of maintaining a successful middle school once it has been implemented. These methods and strategies are illustrated with a detailed example of how one school district planned and implemented a middle school concept in a school district that previously provided traditional junior high schools.

Five resources present practical formats that can be used by the reader as he or she goes about the tasks related to the implementation and maintenance of a middle school. An excellent annotated bibliography is included, to which the reader can turn if more specific, detailed, curricular or structural information is desired.

Anyone who is thinking of going to a middle school structure and implementing a middle school philosophy will find this book of great value, as will others who are currently operating middle schools.

JERRY J. HERMAN
JANICE L. HERMAN
Series Co-Editors

Preface

Schools will be different tomorrow, next month, and next year. Change is inevitable. The challenge (and opportunity) of the school leader is to anticipate the change, create an awareness level of the impending change, and use the available resources to maximize the opportunity. The purpose of this book is to assist school administrators, teachers, and citizens in making a successful transition from a junior high school to a middle school. Emphasis is placed on leading and facilitating the process of transition. It is a book on process (how to) rather than content (what is). An excellent source of books and journal articles concerning the elements of a middle-level school is contained in the annotated bibliography.

This book is divided into five chapters. Chapter 1 provides an example of how one junior high school faculty and administration made the transition to a middle school. Chapter 2 reviews the history and current research of the middle-level reform. The third chapter reviews strategies related to change and conflict. Leadership skills and vision building are examined in the fourth chapter, and information about monitoring progress and recommendations for sustaining the transition process are contained in Chapter 5. Charts related to the transition process are included in the resources section.

The goal of this book is to provide school leaders (both teachers and administrators) with the knowledge and awareness of how a successful transition can take place. It is a book about working with educators and parents in a process that is open, positive, and rewarding to all involved.

Changing from one philosophical perspective to another—in this situation, from a junior high philosophy to a middle-level school philosophy—is a journey rather than a goal. Reaching agreement on a vision statement for a middle-level school is critical, but it is only one step toward improving the educational experience for early adolescent students.

JACK A. MCKAY

About the Author

Jack A. McKay is an Associate Professor and Chair of the Department of Educational Administration at the University of Nebraska at Omaha. He also served as Chair of the Department of Educational Administration at the University of the Pacific in Stockton, California. While in California, he was directly involved in the statewide middle school reform efforts coordinated through the California State Department of Education. He was also instrumental in creating a statewide research consortium interested in networking with regard to the middle-level reform efforts in California.

Prior to teaching and administering at the collegiate level, Dr. McKay was a school administrator in Washington State for 19 years. He was a strong advocate and facilitator of middle-level reform and had direct experience in facilitating the transition from junior high to middle-level schools. He has published several articles on systemwide restructuring, special interest groups, action research, and the superintendency.

Dr. McKay received his MA in educational leadership from Central Washington University. His Ed.D. from Washington State University concentrated on school leadership and governance.

The Journey Toward a
Middle-Level School

How does a group of educators move toward successful implementation of the concepts of a middle-level school? Following is an example of how one school district responded to a problem and an opportunity. The district in this example had two junior high schools, Grades 7 through 9, and one high school. Due to changing demographics of the community, enrollment in the elementary grades was declining. For some educators, the declining enrollment was seen as the beginning of the end of a school system recognized for innovative practices, quality instructional practices, and solid academic programs. For others, it was seen as an opportunity to explore and possibly try some emerging ideas to improve the schooling experience, particularly for early adolescent students.

The Junior High School

The two junior high schools were successful in preparing most students for the high school experience. There was good student participation in after-school activities and athletics. Most students did well academically and made the transition to the high school with little difficulty. In fact, high school faculty were complimentary about how well the junior high school faculty were preparing students for the more rigorous academics and competitive athletics, music, and drama. Faculty and parents were proud of their junior high schools. Unfortunately, with declining enrollments, there were the inevitable discussions about closing one of the junior high schools and several elementary schools.

Phase 1: Problems and Opportunities

The superintendent called a meeting of the junior high principals and other central office administrators to discuss future enrollment trends and the possibility of closing some schools. It was decided that the most effective way to reorganize the district was to consolidate the two junior high schools. These discussions evolved into some serious considerations of a middle-level grade structure. Because no one appreciates surprises (particularly school board members, parents, and teachers), there were meetings at the building level about some of the realignment alternatives and resulting staffing implications. In anticipation of community unrest about closing some of the elementary schools and one junior high school, parent meetings also were held to discuss possible alternatives. Generally, elementary school parents were more vocal about protecting their neighborhood elementary schools than about closing one of the junior high schools.

The formal and informal discussions of new grade alignments created a high level of anxiety among the faculty, administrators, and parents. There were discussions about the educational philosophy, the grouping practices, and the curriculum content at the middle-level school. Under the surface, however, there were far more serious issues related to changing teaching assignments, school philosophy, and the classroom instructional practices. These issues all related directly to one's core beliefs about teaching and student learning. There was a general feeling that teachers were losing professional autonomy and academic freedom. Teachers' concerns about teaching subjects out of their fields of expertise was the major issue facing administrators. The middle-level concepts, such as the core curriculum and interdisciplinary team teaching, were in direct conflict with the instructional practices of the junior high school. If transition from the junior high school to a middle-level school was to be successful, ways had to be found to convince faculty and parents that the middle-level concepts would be better for students and professionally rewarding for teachers.

Educators in the district entered into a series of intense debates about some of the core values of middle-level schooling: teaching subject matter versus teaching the core curriculum; emphasis on the basic subjects versus an exploratory curriculum; athletics versus intramurals; and block scheduling versus the seven-period day. Parents also became emotionally involved with discussions about the placement of the sixth graders with eighth graders, and the ninth graders attending school with juniors and seniors. Along with faculty tension and the anxiety associated with the middle-level concepts, many faculty and parents had emotional investments in the continued success of the traditional junior high schools (i.e., subject matter courses, interscholastic activities, school dances, etc.). Would the middle-level concepts be strong enough to overcome the investment in the junior high school and the resistance to change?

Phase 2: Philosophy and Theory

The superintendent, with school board involvement, created the Middle Level Coordinating Committee (MLCC). The primary purpose of this advisory committee was to organize, communicate, and facilitate the development of recommendations for early adolescent students. The MLCC included four parents representing Grades 5 through 8, six teachers representing the middle-level grades, and the two middle-level school administrators.

The MLCC was provided with secretarial assistance and funding to visit other schools and to hire consultants on middle-level education. The MLCC selected a nationally recognized professor who had expertise in strategic planning to facilitate the transition process. There was no top-down mandate or ready-made, best-way solution presented to the MLCC. The MLCC was responsible for developing recommendations on ways to improve the educational experience for adolescent students.

One of the first tasks of the MLCC was to form 10 subcommittees to investigate a variety of issues and concerns related to the needs of early adolescent students. The subcommittees were established with four and eight members, each representing the school board, administrators, teachers, support staff, or parents. The subcommittees were the following:

1. The Vision Committee was established to develop the vision statement. A vision statement should contain the beliefs about the students, the purpose of schooling, and the outcomes for which students would be held accountable. Each of the remaining subcommittees included the vision statement as part of their findings and recommendations (see Chapter 4: Leadership and Vision Building).

2. The Core Subjects Committee was responsible for studying and reporting findings on the content of language arts, math, social studies, and science. This committee studied how subjects should be delivered to the students in a manner that was consistent with the vision of the school (see Chapter 2: The Emergence of the Middle-Level School).

3. The Instructional Practices Committee was charged with the responsibility of studying and reporting findings on the most effective instructional practices for early adolescent students. Such practices as cooperative learning, small- and large-group instruction, role playing, and computer-assisted instruction were considered.

4. The Exploratory Activities Committee was responsible for studying and developing recommendations for students who would explore and participate in art, music, arts and crafts, home economics, and industrial arts activities in the middle grades.

5. The Physical Education and Athletics Committee was charged with the responsibility for investigating the students' physical exercise and health education needs. This committee also addressed the issue of intramural and interscholastic activities for the middle grades.

6. The Guidance Committee's charge was to report findings on how the students received regular and quality contact with adults. This committee addressed how a strong ad-

vising program would be integrated into the daily lives of the students.

7. The Library and Instructional Support Services Committee was charged with the task of developing a library and multimedia instructional material center for both students and faculty. They addressed the question, "How will the library be integrated to be the center of the total learning environment?"

8. The Social Activities Committee was responsible for reporting the findings concerning activities designed to provide adolescent students with social development.

9. The Progress Reporting Committee was responsible for designing a process that conveyed to students, parents, educators, and citizens the academic, physical, and emotional growth during the middle grades.

10. The Daily Schedule Committee was charged with investigating and recommending the daily schedule. The daily schedule needed to be designed to accommodate blocks of time for the core curriculum, team teaching within the core curriculum, the advising programs, and a variety of exploratory activities being recommended by the other subcommittees.

Monitoring the ongoing progress of the subcommittees and ensuring the sharing of information with all interested groups were the primary responsibilities of the MLCC. The MLCC was also responsible for providing resources, such as released time for teachers to meet; travel funds for committee members to visit other schools; secretarial assistance to assemble, print, and distribute reports; and assistance in accessing research on middle-level schooling located in university libraries and electronic databases. The MLCC also had the responsibility of publishing timely newsletters for educators, parents, and citizens and of establishing timelines for reporting subcommittee findings and recommendations.

The final task of the subcommittees was to report their findings and recommendations to the MLCC. The MLCC then had the responsibility of evaluating and finalizing its findings and then presenting its recommendations to the school board. The subcommittees completed their assignments within 6 months, and the MLCC presented its findings and recommendations to the school board within 8 months. With the approval of the school board, the MLCC had completed its assigned tasks and was dissolved. After school board approval, student and parent orientation meetings were held at the elementary schools.

Following the school board approval of the recommendation to move forward with the middle-level concepts, the superintendent, with school board approval, appointed faculty, administrators, and parents to the Middle Level Implementation Committee (MLIC). The MLIC was responsible for the planning of the opening of the middle-level school.

Phase 3: Bridging Theory and Practice

The "bridging theory and practice" year coincided with the second year of the transition phase from a junior high school to a middle school. The primary purpose of the "bridging" year was to provide administrators and faculty with the opportunity to develop plans to implement the middle-level school concepts. A series of staff development workshops was planned that dealt directly with the concepts of the following: the core curriculum, interdisciplinary teaming, the daily schedule, the advisor-advisee program, the exploratory courses, and student activity programs. The purpose of the workshops was to discuss and finalize the implementation of the concepts of middle-level education. Consultants were hired to review the concepts and to facilitate the planning process for implementation. The primary concerns during the bridging phase were to explore opportunities and to keep everyone informed about what was happening in preparation for beginning a new middle-level school.

Another concern during the bridging phase of the transition was informing and gaining feedback from teachers, support staff, and parents about the kind of schooling experiences planned for students attending the middle-level school. This phase was an opportunity for teachers to explore different instructional practices. Decisions also had to be made about the pace of implementation. Some practitioners have estimated up to 10 years are needed to institutionalize all of the middle-level concepts.

Transition Strategies

Following are some of the strategies used to make the transition from a junior high school to a middle-level school:

- Continual communication with school board, faculty, and parents (particularly parents in the elementary grades)
- Continual development of strategies to increase the awareness of faculty and parents about early adolescent needs
- Regular visits to other schools that have implemented similar programs for middle-level grade students
- Continual monitoring of the vision statement and other transition activities to ensure that the new middle-level school was progressing toward meeting the needs of early adolescent students

With an atmosphere of openness and risk-taking, the first year was seen as an opportunity to try a new approach to teaching. It also presented faculty with an opportunity to find out if teaching at the middle grades was professionally appropriate.

Summary

An example of how one group of educators worked through the transition from a junior high to a middle-level school was divided into three phases: (a) problems and opportunities, (b) collecting and sharing information, and (c) planning and implementation. As with any change, there was anxiety and frustration about what was happening or allegedly going to happen. There was occasional conflict about how to put the middle-grade concepts into practice; for some faculty, it was an exploration of new teaching strategies, but for others, it was the beginning of a period of tension and frustration about the pending changes in teaching, relations with students, and relations with other teachers.

The Emergence of the Middle-Level School

In 1918, the highly influential report *Cardinal Principles of Secondary Education* by the Commission on the Reorganization of Secondary Education (1918) gave a push for the junior high school. The commission recommended that the second 6 years of schooling should be divided into two phases. The junior high school period should place emphasis on attempts to help the student explore aptitudes and make some choices about future work. The senior high school period was to place emphasis on job training.

The junior high school era was to be a gradual introduction to departmental (subject matter) instruction, some choice of subjects (under careful guidance), promotion based on grades, prevocational choices, and a social organization that would promote the development of personal responsibility and the welfare of the group.

In 1920, the junior high school was designed to offer a program of study with more breadth and richness than the traditional elementary school. The junior high school would allegedly offer better trained teachers, improved facilities, and a more appropriate student activities program. Most junior high schools were intended to be more responsive to the early adolescent; however, most appeared to become mini-high schools.

The junior high school, like most school reform efforts, suffered when taken to extremes. Criticism of the junior high school centered around the tendency to mirror the senior high school. During the early years of the junior high school movement, there continued to be specialization of subject matter, abstract and formal lectures, emphasis on college preparation, interscholastic athletics, marching bands, and formal dances. These characteristics all contributed to the feeling that the junior high school was similar to the high school.

According to Lewis (1992), the junior high movement was an effort to separate the early adolescents and to provide programs uniquely designed for them. However, a knowledge base was not available to sustain the uniqueness of the junior high school, and the movement gradually moved toward a subject orientation like that of the traditional high school.

In reviewing the growth of the junior high school, one needs to put schools in the social context that existed during the first half of the 20th century. The United States was emerging as a world power with military victories in the Spanish-American War and World War I. The nation was fast becoming the industrial and financial capital of the world. There was a cult of efficiency: assembly lines, employee specialization, bureaucratic management styles, hierarchy of power, and the chain of command. All of these factors influenced the structure of most organizations and transferred over to schooling. Applying the industrial paradigm to education (and particularly to the junior high school) was a logical step in organizing administrators and teachers to efficiently teach children.

Even before the beginning of the end of the industrial age—generally considered the late 1950s and early 1960s—the need to re-examine the schooling of early adolescents became a concern. It was believed by Mac Iver (1989) that the declining academic achievement among adolescents was due to the mismatch between the developmental needs of these students and the educational environment. This was found to be especially true for disadvantaged students who were dropping out of school.

The Carnegie Council on Adolescent Development (1989), in *Turning Points*, addressed the mismatch between schooling and the needs of early adolescent students as follows:

The world is being rapidly transformed by science and technology in ways that have profound significance for our economic well-being and for a democratic society. Work will require much more technical competence and a great deal of flexibility. In the years immediately ahead, the national cohort of young people will be smaller than in recent decades. Fewer college-age students will enter the workforce. We need to develop the talent of all our people if this nation is to be economically competitive and socially cohesive in the different world of the next century.

To do so, we must take advantage of the neglected opportunity provided by the fascinating period of early adolescence, ages 10 to 15 years. This is a time not only of inordinate vulnerability, but an exceptional chance for constructive interventions that can have lifelong influence.

The onset of adolescence is a critical period of biological and psychological change for the individual. These years are highly formative for behavior patterns in education and health that have enduring significance. Adolescence is typically characterized by exploratory behavior, much of which is developmentally appropriate and socially adaptive for most young people.

There is a crucial need to help adolescents at this early age to acquire durable self-esteem, flexible and inquiring habits of mind, reliable and relatively close human relationships, a sense of belonging in a valued group, and a sense of usefulness in some way beyond self. They need to find constructive expressions of their inherent curiosity and exploratory energy, and they need a bias for making informed, deliberate decisions—especially on matters that have large consequences, such as their educational futures and drug use. (pp. 12-13)

Another factor contributing to the increased interest in early adolescent education was the limited amount of information available. Early research emphasis was on elementary and high school education. This neglect of middle-level schooling is easily seen in the lack of agreement about which grades to include in the middle-level schools.

The challenge for educators is to create a middle-level school that meets the needs of the young adolescent. The middle-level school must change to cope with the requirements of a new era—to give its students a decent chance in life and to help them fulfill their potential.

Characteristics of the Middle-Level School

The restructuring of the middle grades has been motivated by both positive and negative factors. Clark and Valentine (1981) believed middle-level programs benefit students in three primary areas: organizational structure, scope and sequence of curriculum content, and methods of instruction.

Experienced educators have acknowledged that the real motivators for change toward the middle-level school are often based on the availability of classroom space. Where do you put the relatively "vulnerable and impressionable" ninth graders or where do you put the "worldly" and more mature sixth graders? This placement of ninth graders and sixth graders is a prime example of the uniqueness of the early adolescent. A concise review of the major differences between a middle-level school and a junior high school is provided in Table 2.1.

Middle-Level School Theory

The theory to support the middle grade movement is based on the belief that early adolescents' academic, social, and emotional needs are best served by an educational experience that is met by neither the elementary school format nor the high school environment. The schooling experience for early adolescence should include a set of concepts in the areas of (a) guidance, (b) transitional and orientation activities, (c) flexibility in scheduling of the school day, (d) the core curriculum, (e) interdisciplinary team teaching, (f) instructional strategies, (g) intramural activities, and (h) exploratory

TABLE 2.1 Comparing the Middle-Level School to Junior High School

Topic	Middle-Level School	Junior High School
Grade structure	Usually sixth through eighth.	Usually seventh through ninth.
Ages	11 to 15 years old.	12 to 16 years old.
Grouping students	Heterogeneous grouping. Opportunities are provided for students to learn from and to accept peers from different socioeconomic backgrounds.	Ability grouping based on academic achievement test results.
School subjects	Core subjects are integrated and taught by a team of teachers. A wide variety of elective courses is available for students to develop their interests.	Departmentalized by subject matter.
Advising	Teachers in advisor/advisee relationships. Organized to provide time for adults to give advice on academic, personal, and social matters.	Counselors assigned students based on grade level, alphabetical order, or gender.
Extracurricular activities	Intramurals incorporated into the school day so that all students have an opportunity to participate.	Interscholastic athletics, usually after school.
Daily schedule	Blocks of time for interdisciplinary study.	Six or seven periods of equal length each day.
Teachers' schedule	Interdisciplinary teaming.	Single-subject assignments.
Teachers' background	Core curriculum, student centered, advising responsibilities, team teaching, tendency toward elementary school.	Subject orientation, tendency toward high school philosophy.

courses. The theory of middle-level education is that with the appropriate experiences, students will become more effective persons, more effective participants with other students and adults, and stronger academically.

The theory of middle-level schooling is based on developmental psychology and effective schools research. Researchers have found that a student's brain grows in phases; therefore, early adolescent students have different capacities for learning than their brothers and sisters in high school. Toepfer (1988) found that advanced placement is not always better for introducing high-school-level academic challenges to middle-level students. The assumption that early adolescents can achieve if they just "try harder" is being questioned. Readiness, not effort, is a critical factor in academic growth. For many early adolescents, concrete operational tasks may be relatively easy, whereas abstract intellectual challenges create only frustration and inappropriate labeling. Implications from this research would indicate that early adolescents need concrete, hands-on experiences that sustain interest and facilitate the process of abstract thinking.

Effective Schools Research

Effective schools research also has had an impact on the emerging importance of middle-level schooling. The characteristics of effective schools have been developed to help educators monitor progress toward improving schools. Following is a list of effective school characteristics developed by Levine and Lezotte (1990). (See Resource A for the information in a chart format.)

1. *Productive school climate and culture.* There is an orderly environment, faculty commitment to a shared and articulated mission, and a problem-solving orientation. The faculty models cohesion, collaboration, consensus, communications, collegiality, and mechanisms for input into decision making. Finally, there is a schoolwide emphasis on recognizing positive performance.

2. *Focus on student acquisition of central learning skills.* There is maximum availability and use of time for learning with an emphasis on mastery of central learning skills.

3. *Appropriate monitoring of student progress.*

4. *Practice-oriented staff development at the school site.*

5. *Outstanding leadership.* Principals are vigorous in the selection and replacement of teachers. They are mavericks in their orientation and willing to buffer teachers from influential external agents that threaten to reduce effectiveness or commitment. They frequently monitor classrooms and school activities. They spend a great deal of time and energy on school improvement actions, support their teachers, acquire resources, model superior instructional leadership, and ensure the availability and effective use of instructional support personnel.

6. *Genuine parent involvement.*

7. *Effective instructional arrangements and implementation.* There are successful grouping and related organizational arrangements, appropriate pacing and alignment, active and enriched learning experiences, effective teaching practices, an emphasis on higher order learning in assessing instructional outcomes, coordination in curriculum and instruction practices, easy availability of abundant and appropriate instructional materials, and adaptable classrooms.

8. *High operationalized expectations and requirements for students.*

9. Other characteristics of effective schools include (a) a student's sense of efficacy or futility, (b) the use of multicultural instruction, (c) sensitivity and personal and social development programs for students, and (d) rigorous and equitable student promotion policies and practices.

Components of the Middle-Level Grades

According to Alexander and George (1981), the six essential program concepts of a middle-level school are as follows:

1. *Guidance.* The guidance program should provide an adult who has the time and responsibility for each student, assuring familiarity and continuity in providing advice on academic, personal, and social matters. The components of a middle-level guidance program are
   - Adults (teachers and administrators) who work with a small group of students during the middle school years to establish a stable and long-term relationship with each student
   - A well-planned sequence of activities to develop and nurture the adult-student relationship
   - A school schedule that enables the small group to meet each school day throughout the school year
2. *Transition and articulation.* Schools should ensure a smooth transition between elementary and high school by orienting students and providing close articulation and coordination of learning experiences. Examples of transition and articulation are
   - The orientation of students and parents before, during, and after the transition from the elementary grades
   - The inclusion of activities that aid the students' increasing responsibilities for decision making in such areas as academic, social, and emotional situations during the transition from the middle-level grades to high school
3. *Interdisciplinary teaming and block scheduling.* The daily schedule should feature blocks of instructional time during which interdisciplinary teams of teachers provide appropriate learning experiences for their students. Other characteristics of teaming and block scheduling are
   - The creation of heterogeneous teams, typically between 100 and 150 students
   - The creation of interdisciplinary teams of teachers in areas such as math, science, social studies, and language arts
   - A schedule of common planning times for the interdisciplinary teacher team
   - The development of a schedule within the block of time that can be altered to provide for the regrouping of students

4. *Appropriate teaching strategies.* A variety of teaching strategies that have been shown to be particularly effective with students of this age group should be used. Other characteristics of appropriate teaching strategies are
   - The adaptation of instructional strategies to the characteristics of the learner and sensitivity to the individual's levels of intellectual development
   - Noting the relationship between the content and actual life situations
   - Built-in flexibility to meet the varying developmental needs and learning styles of students by using such strategies as mastery learning, tutoring, critical thinking skills, cooperative learning, computers and related technology information, and hands-on materials

5. *Exploratory curriculum.* Schools should offer a wide range of exploratory or elective courses for students to develop their interests. All students should have the opportunity to participate in intramural athletics. Examples of an exploratory curriculum are
   - The development of short courses in nontraditional, high-interest areas such as arts and crafts, music and drama, electronics and computers, cooking and gardening, and photography and architecture
   - The provision of intramural athletics and club activities for students during the school day to provide ample opportunities for participation

6. *Appropriate core curriculum and learning skills.* A core of learning experiences appropriate to the middle-level phase of schooling should be required of all students, and students should master learning skills needed for future study. Examples of core curriculum activities are
   - A focus on culture, science, and the humanities
   - An established set of expectations for proficiency in reading, speaking, and listening
   - Emphasis on the rights of self and others as well as responsibilities as citizens

The Curriculum in the Middle-Level Grades

Developers of the middle-level curriculum must recognize that although students will be working toward the same outcomes, some will take longer to achieve the outcomes and will need extra support through unique instructional strategies and materials. Those students who meet outcomes more quickly must be allowed the flexibility to move ahead to new challenges.

Systematic, systemwide curriculum planning is needed to develop curricular alternatives appropriate for middle-level students. A systematic curriculum positively affects student learning; those alternatives must encourage individual progress toward desired curriculum goals. This entails reconceptualizing middle-level curriculum functions in terms of the needs of a contemporary and emerging society and based on a recognition of the different educational needs of young adolescents.

The following concerns were presented by Beane (1990) to help guide teachers and administrators considering the middle-level curriculum:

> If the middle-level school is to be based upon the characteristics of early adolescence, then the curriculum ought to be redesigned along developmentally appropriate lines rather than simply a slightly revised version of the traditional high school curriculum. Being sensitive to early adolescent characteristics is only part of "reform." The "how to teach" question must be accompanied by a "what do we teach and learn?" question. (p. 5)

The curriculum should consist of thematic units whose organizing centers are drawn from the intersecting concerns of early adolescents and issues in the larger world. If the middle-level school curriculum is to prepare youth for the future, the curriculum should develop intellectual skills and an understanding of humankind that will permit the student to gather information, organize it in a meaningful fashion, evaluate its utility, form reasonable conclusions about it, and plan for individual and collective action.

The Guidance Program

The attention devoted to the guidance services for the unique needs of early adolescent students has always been of major importance from the beginning of the junior high school. According to Noar (1961), the early junior high school guidance program was to meet the following four needs of the early adolescent's emotions:

1. The need for security and affection, which creates a feeling of being wanted and a sense of belonging
2. The need for recognition and reward
3. The need for achievement and success
4. The need for fun and adventure, both educational and recreational

Unlike the high school, where the counselors are basically responsible for guidance services, the middle-level school philosophy is that the responsibilities for guidance are also the obligation of the entire faculty and administration. Guidance is an ongoing activity that incorporates opportunities for personal development within the instructional program. The responsibilities of teachers and administrators in advising at the middle school are suggested below:

1. Establish a caring relationship with individual students
2. Be available to students to discuss concerns and interests
3. Confer with students and parents (communication link between school, home, and community)
4. Assist students in obtaining information about school activities
5. Serve as a first-line source of referral (e.g., counselors, nurses, other specialists)
6. Serve as an academic expert and student advocate
7. Provide social and emotional education to students
8. Provide a "sounding board" by assisting students in working out problems
9. Conduct group guidance activities

Grouping Students in the Middle-Level Grades

Homogeneous grouping of students based on ability has been a well-accepted practice in Grades 5 through 9 for many decades. Teachers believed that grouping or tracking students based on academic ability would provide them with more opportunities to efficiently structure lessons to meet the needs and abilities of the particular group of students.

Johnston and Markle (1983) concluded from their research that although a majority of teachers believe that ability grouping improves effectiveness, the practice has deleterious effects on teacher expectations and instructional practices, especially for lower ability-grouped students, in the areas of perceptions of self and others and academic performance. Furthermore, ability grouping limits opportunities for students to learn from and accept peers of different social and economic backgrounds. It may perpetuate the notions of superior and inferior classes of persons.

The Student

Educators are well aware of the diversity of physical, social, emotional, and intellectual stages of development of students in the middle-level grades. Diversity, not uniformity, is the norm. This diversity of students takes place within an environment of individual differences among teachers and administrators who have differing points of view about curriculum and instructional strategies. Following is a review of the typical characteristics of early adolescent students.

Physical Development

Age is not a major factor in determining when rapid physical growth takes place. During the 10- to 15-year-old age range, girls may grow taller than boys. Another characteristic is the uneven development of bone and muscle structure, resulting in a lack of coordination. The physical growth of students varies more in Grades 7 and 8 than in other years.

Social Development

Social development ranges from a strong dependence by adolescents on the home and family to those who turn to peers as sources for standards and models of behavior. Group membership is a strong social need, and students will go to great lengths to acquire it and respond readily to what they see as peer pressure.

Emotional Development

Feelings of inadequacy, superiority or inferiority, and independence from parents are common among adolescents. These feelings are different at times for themselves and between themselves and others. They struggle with self-concept and sex role identification. They have a short attention span and relatively shallow thinking powers.

Intellectual Development

Intellectual development ranges from limited thinking skills to formal abstract thinking. The right and left brain development and growth periods lead to a wide range of academic ability among students.

Teachers in the Middle-Level School

The uniqueness of the middle-level grades is further exemplified when the faculty is described. Not only are the students characterized by a diversity in social, physical, and academic maturity, but the faculty is also marked by differences. Middle-level faculty range in philosophy from an elementary school perspective of the self-contained, child-centered approach to instruction and social development to the high school philosophy of departmentalization and a subject-centered approach.

Further diversity of middle-level faculty members is marked by their career stages and aspirations. Some faculty may feel misplaced and trapped in the middle grades because of limited opportunities to be "up at the high school." Others would prefer to be at the elementary school, where there is the nostalgia of strong parent support and docile students.

Bringing together teachers, some of whom feel they are not appropriately assigned nor trained to deal with early adolescents, coupled with additional teachers who have a limited commitment to the philosophy of the middle-level grades, leaves a school administrator with some major challenges. Certainly, the school environment can only be compounded by a school leader who has an ambivalent commitment and vision about the schooling of early adolescent students.

Summary

The intent of the original junior high school and emergence of a renewed interest in the middle-level school were summarized in this chapter. Although the junior high school has been seen as a positive step toward meeting the unique needs of the early adolescent student, the efforts generally fall short. Now, with additional research and commitment to meeting the needs of these students, the middle-level school has a stronger sense of vision and purpose to overcome the operationalization of the traditional junior high school. The next chapter is a review of the strategies and changes that need to be considered when contemplating the transition to the middle-level school.

The Two Cs:
Change and Conflict

The changing of a junior high school faculty, support staff, students, and parents is a major event. Although the change primarily affects the middle-level grades, it also has implications for elementary and high school teachers. Change is not a refined process; however, under proper conditions and with appropriate leadership, the odds of it being successful and lasting can be increased significantly. With change in any organization, there will be stress on all members. Machiavelli (1952), when giving advice to the Prince, said:

> It must be considered that there is nothing more difficult to carry out, nor more doubtful of success, nor more dangerous to handle, than to initiate a new order of things. For the reformer has enemies in all those who profit by the old order, and only lukewarm defenders in all those who would profit by the new order, this lukewarmness arising partly from fear of their adversaries, who have the laws in their favor; and partly from the incredulity of mankind, who do not truly believe in anything new until they have had actual experience of it. (p. 49)

Conditions for Change

Harvey (1990) found that certain conditions must exist before successful change can take place. Successful change requires

- Commitment to the change by the leaders of a critical mass of stakeholders
- Clear vision of what the school will look like when the change is completed
- Clear-cut strategic goals, objectives, and indicators of progress toward the vision
- Understandable plans of how the changes will improve the organization
- Training of those individuals who are to initiate and/or manage the change
- Adequate time, finances, materials, and human resources to enhance the probability of successful change taking place
- High-quality, comprehensive, and frequent two-way communications
- Ability to adjust the plans if changes are required during the initiation and implementation stages
- Recognition of good work and celebrating the reaching of important objectives

Politics of Change

Attempting to create change in an organization and, in this situation, changing to the middle-level school concepts can be a dangerous activity in a political sense. The parties involved include students, parents, taxpayers, school board members, central office administrators, teachers, and administrators in other buildings. Each of these groups has different needs and aspirations. They also have a degree of comfort in the current school routines and priorities (see annotated bibliography for an excellent book on change: Harvey, 1990).

Lasting change in schools should have the following characteristics:

1. Changes are presented in a way that can be implemented.
2. Changes are focused at the building level.
3. Changes are acceptable to those involved.
4. Changes are compatible with the organizational structure.
5. Changes are supported with time and funding.
6. Changes are supported with sense of ownership.
7. Changes are supported with opportunities for learning skills.
8. Changes are supported with partnership with other schools.

Sources of Resistance to Change

Most of us do not seek out change. We understand the security and benefit of staying with the known because we do not know the payoff for choosing the unknown. Rather than seeing resistance to change as negative, it may be better to accept it as a natural tendency. People resist change unless there is a clear benefit to them. The benefit to the changer (the sender) is irrelevant; rather, the benefit to the changee (the receiver) must be taken into account.

In a school or in any organization, there should be some degree of stress. If there is no stress and strain, there will likely be no change. Learning new information or creating something will result in some stress. People seek information when they realize the information will be helpful. Likewise, people create new products and services after the stress caused by a lack of something. The challenge for the changer is to develop the need and facilitate the process of having the changee understand the need to gain new information or to use a new product or service.

Conditions for Successful Change

If the changer wants to move the changee from one condition or belief to another, three steps should take place. The first is unfreezing, or being open and receptive to new information. The second is moving toward accepting the new information, and the third is refreezing, or reestablishing the new information as the most valid. The refreezing is the easiest. The moving phase takes planning, but it is not as difficult as the process of unfreezing—having the changee open to new information that may alter his or her original beliefs. For the changee to be open to new information, three conditions need to be present: strain, value, and potential. Strain is the less-than-satisfactory condition. There has to be a positive value to a new place—not just a value to move away from a negative place or position. Finally, there has to be a potential for success. The changee must believe that the proposed change will work and that it is possible to change beliefs. Finally, the change, to be more than a fad or whim, must have ownership among the changees. This means collaborative activities before and during the process of change.

There are three general strategies used to bring about change: (a) strength and power—it is my way or the highway, (b) new facts and information—it just makes sense, and (c) the payoff—it meets the needs and wants of those involved.

The use of strength and power with the threat of "or else" creates resistance and cynical attitudes. The use of facts and figures (e.g., university research studies) seldom creates the environment for change. The rational approach to change is one of the most effective methods, but it is also the most difficult and most time consuming. The changer must accurately identify the needs and wants of the changee. Only when the needs and wants of the changee are identified and matched with the proposed changes will the process of unfreezing, moving, and refreezing take place.

Barriers to Successful Change

The following list of questions developed by Harvey (1990) should be considered when planning the process of change. Facilitators of the process of changing a junior high school to a middle-level school will need answers to the following list of barriers (see Resource C for the chart format of the change barriers).

- Lack of ownership

    What strategies will bring people together to explore the middle-level grade educational concepts?

    What activities will bring about participation and enthusiasm on how middle-level grade programs can be implemented?

- Lack of benefit

  What are the rewards for teachers, parents, and students—those who are affected by the proposed middle-level school concepts?

  Are the rewards short or long term, tangible or intangible, and professional or personal for teachers, parents, and students?

- Lack of time or funding resources

  How are the changes going to affect the already limited resources of time, space, and funding?

  How will the change to a middle-level school format provide more time and resources to do a better job of educating students?

- Lack of support from superiors

  How can the school board, district, and building administrators accept and actively support the middle-level grade concepts?

  What strategies are available to explain the middle-level grade concepts?

  What are the benefits of middle-level grade concepts to the district office administrators, the school board, and other building administrators?

- Support systems

  How will the anxiety of being the first to try something new be addressed?

  What kind of support will be available to assist the different groups involved in the change to the middle-level grade concepts?

  Who will coordinate the support needed by the different groups that may face pressures to return to the former methods (e.g., school board members, parents, other administrators, students)?

- Lack of security

  How will those involved in the change to the middle-level grade concepts be assured of job security and professional autonomy—two primary concerns of teachers?

What staff development activities will be available to enhance the teaching and advising skills needed to carry out the middle-level grade concepts?

How will the change from departmentalization to an interdisciplinary core of subjects be addressed?

- Counter to cultural norms

What customs and traditions of the junior high school will be incorporated into the middle-level school culture?

How will the cultural norms of the students, parents, and faculty be adapted to the middle-level grade concepts (e.g., orientation, graduation, social activities, and athletics)?

- Lack of order or control

What strategies will be in place to reduce the possibility of the feeling of things being out of control?

What strategies will be in place to reduce the fear that there will be no control over what teachers teach and how students behave?

- Pushed on the group by the principal or superintendent; the decision has already been made about changing to a middle-level school

What strategies will be used to counter the perception of having the answers (before the problem is clearly understood)?

How will the feeling of superiority (e.g., supporting middle-level school concepts) and inferiority (e.g., supporting the junior high school concepts) be reduced to a minimum?

- Unequal distribution of information

What strategies will be used to sustain the flow of information about the change to the middle-level school?

How will all those involved in the conversion to the middle-level school concepts feel included in the flow of information so that there are no surprises?

- Lack of recognition

What strategies will be used to give recognition to those assuming leadership and risk taking in the process of moving from a junior high to a middle-level school?

What strategies will be used to provide opportunities for recognition to those who once opposed or were skeptical of the conversion?

- Too much change and too fast

  What strategies will be used in planning the pace of the change from the junior high to the middle-level school?

  How will the small but progressive steps taken in the change process be recognized and celebrated?

- Fear of failure

  What steps will be taken to include and recognize the people who resist the change to a middle-level school?

  How will participants be reassured with positive support during and after the change process?

  What strategies will be used to counter the negative comments that will surface during the change from a junior high school to a middle-level school?

- Balanced organizational structure

  How will the balance between a highly centralized and a highly decentralized structure be maintained (e.g., between too much direction and too much participation)?

Responding to Conflict

When there is change, there will be conflict. Conflict is a natural part of the change process. Conflict results from vested interests in the junior high school concepts, the middle-level grade philosophy, the personalities of faculty and administrators, and new teaching and advising assignments. Conflict is normal and can even be a positive part of school improvement. Knowing how to anticipate, respond, and facilitate the management of conflict is one of the more important skills for educational leaders. Managing instead of resolving conflict is emphasized because resolving implies closure, which seldom occurs. Managing conflict is an ongoing process and is more realistic of what happens between people of differing views.

In order to understand conflict and how to appropriately respond when attempting to manage the dispute, it helps to know the typical behavior patterns of the people involved. There are two primary roles in conflict: participant and manager. Participants in conflict are usually single-minded, present their own point of view, make assumptions, are reluctant or unwilling to listen, and are interested only in pursuing their own self-interests. A manager of conflict seeks facts, thinks about the situation from different perspectives, helps people explain their points of view, and looks for solutions to the problem. (For an excellent source for further information on managing conflict, see Crawley, 1992, in the annotated bibliography.)

The following are suggested questions that conflict managers should ask before responding in a conflict situation:

1. What can I do? What do I want? What are my responsibilities?
2. Can I manage this conflict fairly?
3. What are my boundaries?
4. How much of my own personality can I use?
5. Will my style of management fit in with the situation?
6. What resources can I draw on?
7. Do I have the special knowledge to become involved?
8. Do I have the power or authority to act effectively?
9. Is it appropriate for me to be involved in this conflict?
10. What are my relations with each conflicting party?
11. Do I have the time to become involved in this situation?
12. Do I have any experiences on which to draw to help resolve this conflict?

Managing Conflict

Before making the decision to become involved in managing a conflict, five questions should be considered: Have the people put the conflict on hold? Has the role of the conflict manager been explained? Has agreement been sought on how to proceed in trying to manage the conflict? Has a workable agreement been developed? Has acknowledgment of the agreement by all involved been clearly communicated and gained?

An effective conflict manager in an educational environment should have the following skills:

- Impartiality: has a concern about the outcome for both sides
- Listening skills: listens actively and shows empathy
- Trust: shows thoughts and feelings are understood
- Persuasion skills: knows about gestures and body language
- Problem solving: knows the importance of collaborative solutions
- Interaction: uses effective process skills in coping with conflict
- Self-awareness: pays attention to his or her own behavior
- Flexibility: is able to change the process
- Understands people: has experience in dealing with people in conflict
- Professionalism: treats situation seriously, with preparation, and on time
- Balance: is aware of his or her own feelings and feelings of others

Following are some general questions to ask about the conflict situation:

1. What does the initial information about the conflict say?
2. Are there existing procedures and structures to follow?
3. Are there cost and resource limitations?
4. Are there deadlines imposed on either side?
5. How will the resolution affect future efficiency and motivation?
6. Are there other factors that need to be considered?

Following are questions to ask about the parties involved in the conflict:

1. What do I know about them? What do they want?
2. Have they been in similar conflicts in the past?
3. What are their interests, needs, values, beliefs, and principles?
4. Are they reliable, sensitive, intolerant, or difficult?

5. Are there limits to what the people are prepared to accept?
6. Are there strengths, and how are they likely to use them?
7. Are their levels of feelings congruent with events, or exaggerated?
8. How aware are they about the effect of their behavior?
9. Do they have more knowledge of the situation to share?
10. Have the parties acted competently?
11. What is the power balance in the conflict?
12. What relationships did the parties have previous to the conflict?
13. How is the conflict affecting their work?
14. Are others involved in the conflict?

Summary

How change is viewed by the changer and changee, how it is planned and implemented, and how conflict emerges from change have been summarized in this chapter. The leader should be aware of the inevitable conflict that will arise during the phases of change from the routines of the junior high school to the less stable times of implementing the concepts of a middle-level school. The strategies used to manage conflict have been reviewed.

Leadership and Vision Building

The transition from the junior high school to the middle-level school requires a special kind of educational leader. The educational leader must have the ability to lead and manage, possess a vision, and have the ability to influence and motivate others and effectively communicate with others. Information about essential leadership skills for middle-level school leaders, strategies for building a vision, and examples of vision statements for middle-level education is contained in this chapter.

The foundation of middle-level leadership is that it will be a shared role. The middle-level school needs more leadership, not less. Along with middle-level school planning is the expectation that the leader will lead other leaders. Together, the principal and teachers are instructional leaders. The emphasis is exchanging the leader and follower role. Effective leaders have the ability to build their own strengths and the strengths of others, focus on opportunities, and view problems as challenges.

Leadership Definition

Leadership is defined by Rost (1991) as an influence relationship among leaders and collaborators who intend real changes that reflect their mutual purposes. Leadership is seen as a shared responsibility transferred between the participants. The leadership activity is seen as episodic or temporary. Leadership becomes interchangeable during the activity. There may be one leader to facilitate the development of a vision statement and another to be responsible for obtaining closure on the middle-level school concepts.

If the leadership activity in the school is an influence relationship about making real changes, then management of the school is seen as the authority relationship between persons in charge and the members of the group who at that particular time are the followers. Both leadership and management are essential to the improvements and operations of the school. Leadership is needed to establish direction, whereas management is needed to move the organization in the desired direction. Because leadership is episodic, management is the time-consuming duty of the principal. This emerging definition of leadership grows in an environment of self-confidence and trusting relationships. (For additional information on leadership, see Rost, 1991, in the annotated bibliography.)

Leadership for the Middle-Level School

Relating more specifically to middle-level school leadership, Clark and Clark (1989) identified the desired characteristics of leaders attempting to bring about middle-level school reform:

- A passion for middle-level education
- A willingness to share decision making
- A concern for the well-being of all persons in the school
- An opportunity orientation toward problems
- A good self-concept
- A model of school norms
- An awareness of differences between middle and high school students
- An awareness of the importance of continual communications
- An awareness of the sensitivity of early adolescent students and their own process of socializing with other students and adults

- An awareness of the ebb and flow between the willingness to explore and the need to have the stability of the known
- An awareness of the differing demands placed on students because of a changing family structure and resulting moral, social, and ethical dilemmas
- An awareness of the need to provide opportunities for students to have a wide variety of school activities in which to explore, participate, and excel

Leadership and Credibility

An additional skill of middle-level school leaders is the ability to communicate with credibility. When school leaders are perceived to have high credibility and a strong vision, researchers have found that teachers and support staff are proud to tell others that they are part of the school, talk positively with their friends about the school at which they work, see their own values as similar to those of the school, and feel a sense of ownership in the school's future. However, when the leader is perceived to have low credibility, faculty and support staff believe that their colleagues are working only when watched; motivated only by money; saying good things at school, but saying negative things in private; and actively looking for other career opportunities.

Credibility is one of the hardest attributes to earn as a leader and is the most fragile. To build credibility, according to Kouzes and Posner (1993), the leader needs to accomplish the following: (a) know the members; (b) become known to the members; and (c) get to know others as people, not as statistics or numbers in the organization. Credibility is earned over a long period of time, but can be lost relatively quickly.

People want a leader who is trustworthy, competent, dynamic, inspiring, and has a vision of the future. According to Kouzes and Posner (1987), effective leaders demonstrate the following behaviors:

- They challenge the process and are willing to take risks.
- They inspire a shared vision of the future and seek to include others.

- They enable others to act by promoting collaboration.
- They model leadership by setting an example and planning small wins.
- They encourage others by recognizing and celebrating their contributions.

The transition process of changing a junior high school to a middle-level school is more than a declaration and implementation. The successful transition needs a leader, with followers, who can decide on a vision, understand change and conflict, and manage the effective use of resources. Finally, the leader must improve the attributes of credibility and facilitation. (For an excellent source of additional information about building credibility, see Kouzes and Posner, 1993, in the annotated bibliography.)

Vision Building

Even if the middle-level school leader has the essential leadership characteristics, the primary factor in determining the success of the transition of a junior high school faculty and staff to a middle-level school is the development of a vision statement. A vision is a set of agreed-upon beliefs of what the middle-level school is to become. A compelling vision is the key factor of leadership. A leader with a vision has the capacity to create and communicate a view of the desired state of affairs.

The middle-level school leader needs to facilitate the development and communication of the school's vision. A vision is like an idea: It needs nurturing or it will die. It needs constant attention and must be communicated throughout the school and community. A vision statement is in competition with issues and routine operations of the school. Routines are established customs that are sustained by habit and tradition. Because a school's vision statement is a description of what the school will be like in the future, it may be threatening to the people who have vested interests in the current routines and customs. People feel comfortable with routine operational activities and tend to be reluctant to go through the process of building a vision statement.

A clear vision statement, according to Tregoe, Zimmerman, Smith, and Tobia (1989), will accomplish the following:

1. It will develop a sense of control over the school's destiny. Educators have experienced some major changes during the past 10 years, particularly in the areas of personnel management and technology. With a clear vision to guide decision making, the school can remain focused on educational beliefs. New strategies and technology may aid in the process of fulfilling the vision, but they would not change the vision.

2. It will develop an awareness that current success is no guarantee of future success. Leaders need to communicate that sustaining the current operational routines only supports the present environment. Present thinking promotes the myth that things will stay the same in the future. The practice of "operational thinking" is like making decisions about the future by looking through a rearview mirror.

3. It will develop a direction on how to get out of current situations. A well-developed vision is an effective way to help people think about the future rather than dwell on the past history of the school. Developing the vision causes people to decide what has to be done and to start taking actions to help realize the vision. A vision statement provides the clarity of what the educational experience means for everyone in the school.

4. It will develop a common purpose and a sense of teamwork. The vision provides the common bond that holds people together and sets the tone for collaboration and team building.

5. It will develop a plan on how to obtain more resources. With the competition for resources—funds, personnel, time, and so on—preference is given to the school that is clear about its direction and priorities. A leader who explains where the team wants to go and what is needed to get there often is given the resources.

6. It will develop a plan to exploit a major new threat or opportunity. The school's vision can be sustaining through a storm of controversy or it can provide the grace period to analyze the changing environment.

7. It will develop a need to sustain a direction during a change in leadership. In education, there are often changes on the team. The vision provides the direction to hold the team together during

the period of transition of leadership. The vision may change over time, but there is a sense of direction.

A vision is defined as the framework that guides the choices that determine the nature and direction of the school. It is what the teachers and the principal want the school to be. The vision statement is different from the operations of the school. The vision statement is the framework that holds and guides the school. Operations are part of the daily planning and decision making that guide teaching, curriculum development, and a nurturing climate.

Moving From Vision to Implementation

To move a faculty toward implementation of a vision statement, three basic tasks should be developed: articulating the vision; linking the vision to plans and use of resources; and establishing indicators of success, monitoring progress, and resolving conflicts.

The importance of a vision, particularly when moving from a junior high school to a middle-level school setting, is providing a sense of control over the future. The vision statement draws attention to the purpose of the schooling experience and supports the need for careful allocation of limited resources. One of the axioms of leadership is that either one controls the school's destiny or else some other outside forces will control it. The vacuum of leadership will be filled.

If the vision has been collaboratively developed and endorsed by the faculty and community, the leaders have the "earned" authority and responsibility to move toward that vision. The leaders are enfranchised to manage the school while in pursuit of the vision. (For an excellent source of information about vision building, see Tregoe et al., 1989, in the annotated bibliography.)

Pat Riley (1993), the successful basketball coach, found that the great basketball teams had a vision that he called the covenant. Riley believed that the covenant did the following: bound people together, created an equal footing, helped people shoulder their own responsibilities, prescribed terms for the help and support of others, and created a foundation for teamwork.

The strong belief about the covenant for a basketball team can be translated to the importance of a school's vision statement. The following paraphrases Riley's "Rule of the Heart" (1993, p. 58) and applies it to the middle-level school:

> Every middle-level school faculty must decide, very consciously, to uphold the vision statement that represents the best of values—voluntary cooperation, love, hard work, and total concentration on the good of the students. The greatness flowing through the heart of the faculty must be pumped out to all in the entire school and in the community.

Monitoring the Vision

After the vision has been developed and the faculty is moving along a continuum from routinely operating the school toward implementing the vision, there should be continual monitoring of progress. The "keeper of the vision" is the leader. The following questions should be addressed periodically to monitor the progress toward the vision:

1. Is there a common reference to the vision statement throughout the school? This implies a "oneness of mind" about the direction taken by the faculty. The vision statement provides the context for what is done in the school.
2. Have the implications of the vision statement for the formal and informal structure of the school been addressed? This implies an organizational structure that is compatible with the vision statement of the school.
3. Is there consistency between the school's culture and the vision statement? The school's culture is a pattern of norms, values, beliefs, and attitudes that influences individual and group behavior.

Before a vision statement can be fully developed, the basic beliefs and values must be articulated. Time and effort must be taken to develop clear belief statements about the quality of teaching, ethics, professional growth, and the treatment of colleagues, support staff, and parents. These belief statements are critical to the overall success of the transition from the junior high school to the middle-level school.

Linking the Vision to Plans and Resources

The same people that create the vision are the ones who follow through and make the commitment to carry their thinking forward to implementation. The creators of the vision have the background of knowledge and are highly motivated. If only the leader or a small committee of "visionaries" is supporting the vision statement, the momentum of routine will likely overcome the implementation of the new vision. To make the transition from the vision statement to implementation, the following questions should be answered:

1. What is the most appropriate way to group students within the vision? For example, will students be grouped by academic ability, age, or physical or social maturity?

2. How will the student's interests and needs be determined and emphasized? For example, what criteria are needed to determine those needs? When will these new criteria be useful? What are the new resources and efforts, and when will they be needed?

3. For each major change in emphasis, how valid are the underlying assumptions about such concerns as future student enrollment, parental values, financial priorities, elementary and secondary curricula, and instructional priorities?

4. How will the future school's uniqueness be presented to attract students and improve parental support? What are the elementary and high school teaching strategies that influence middle-level teaching?

5. What resources are needed to promote the vision of education in the future middle-level school? For example, when will time be made available for faculty to design new curriculum and instructional materials? Where are the financial resources for such things as staff development programs and information distributed to the community, parents, and students?

6. What are the major planning activities needed to complete the transition to the future middle-level school? For example, what are the timelines and resource needs of the faculty, the students, the parents, the school board, and administrators in the school system before, during, and after the transition phase? What accountability systems and reporting structures will need to be designed and used during and after the transition from a junior high school to a middle-level school?

7. What results can be expected for each of the activities involved in the transition? For example, what criteria should be used to measure the results of progress toward the vision statement about the middle-level school? Who should be involved in designing the measurement criteria? How will the measurement criteria be communicated?

8. Who monitors the overall progress toward the vision of the middle-level school? Who tracks the underlying assumptions that support the vision statement? Who monitors the resolution of conflicts within and between schools?

The questions above have been formatted into a chart and are located in Resource D.

Sustaining the Vision

Sustaining the vision is one of the key responsibilities of the leader. If the vision statement is the "hope" statement of the school, then the leader is the keeper of the hope. The school community—faculty, support staff, students, and parents—have formal and informal communication networks, norms of behavior, and values to support. The vision statement should be a part of the school, the networks, and the shared values of the school community. The vision needs to become part of what everyone is thinking about and doing. Following are some suggested questions to monitor the implementation of the vision:

- Is there a common reference to the vision statement throughout the school? Is the vision incorporated into problem solving, annual and long-term performance objectives, curriculum and instructional strategies, and communications to internal and external groups?

- Have implications of the vision for the formal and informal structures in the school been considered? What structures or routines of the school need to be changed so that the school community can move toward the vision? What indicators would be appropriate to show symmetry in the school?
- Is there consistency between the school's culture and vision? Is the culture of a school reflected in the norms, values, and beliefs about the purpose of schooling and the needs of adolescents?
- Are there ways to measure the effectiveness of the transition from a junior high school to a middle-level school? How are the indicators of transition being measured? Who is responsible for monitoring the change process?
- Are the conflicts and tensions that develop during the transition phase being identified and resolved? How are these issues being managed during the transition phase?
- How is the vision statement being updated and kept current? When is the vision statement reviewed, and under what situations would revision be appropriate?

A vision statement that is respected and credible with the school community will serve as a guide for planning, decision making, and resource allocations. The challenge for the leader is to sustain the interest and shared ownership of the vision.

Summary

The definition and characteristics of leadership have been reviewed in Chapter 4. Special attention has been given to the importance of the leader's role in developing the vision statement.

Sustaining the
Process of Implementation

Monitoring progress of movement along the continuum from the operational or current routines toward the vision statement of an effective middle-level school is the faculty's concern, but the leader's primary responsibility to facilitate. Following is a list of indicators related to the successful transition from the junior high school to the middle-level school.

1. *Development of a vision statement.* There are opportunities for those in the school community to engage in the creation of the vision of an effective school experience for young adolescents.
2. *Grade organization.* The middle-level school contains a grade alignment that has a sound philosophical base that takes into consideration the needs of the early adolescent.
3. *Team planning and teaching.* Emphasis is on using the teachers' strengths through common and collaborative planning experiences.
4. *Interdisciplinary and integrative learning.* There are opportunities for team planning of appropriate student learning

strategies beyond the core areas of learning (e.g., social studies, language arts, math, and science).

5. *Student groupings.* There are opportunities for a variety of student groupings—large and small—depending on the learning activities and ease of student movement between groups.

6. *Flexible in scheduling.* There are opportunities in the daily schedule for flexibility in designing programs to meet the individual needs of students.

7. *Continuous progress.* There is flexibility in promotion in order to meet the individual learning needs and abilities of the students.

8. *Individualized instruction.* There are opportunities for students to have independent learning to develop personal interests.

9. *Instructional materials.* There are opportunities for students to use materials designed to meet their diverse interests.

10. *Basic skills.* There are effective programs for students in need of strengthening basic learning skills and concepts.

11. *Exploration.* There are opportunities for students to explore a wide variety of interests through a strong exploratory program of study and experience.

12. *Creative experiences.* There are opportunities for creative expression through activities in writing, music, art, and drama.

13. *Social development.* There are programs and services that provide guidance in the development of social skills.

14. *Intramural sports.* There are opportunities for all students to develop physically and to promote team spirit and sportsmanship.

15. *Physical development.* There are programs that help students understand the changes of the body during the adolescent years.

16. *Individualized guidance.* There are opportunities for adult assistance to meet the academic, social, and emotional needs of individuals.

17. *Daily discussions with adults.* There are opportunities for students to have daily interactions with an adult both in small groups and individually.
18. *Social development.* There are opportunities for students to identify and learn about appropriate values and the development of those values for future decisions.
19. *Monitoring student achievement.* There are opportunities for frequent feedback to students about progress and also opportunities to provide assistance for addressing shortfalls in individualized academic objectives.
20. *Orientation and transition to and from the middle-level school.* There are opportunities for students to participate in well-planned orientation experiences that move from the self-contained elementary school to the departmentalized high school.
21. *Staff development.* There are opportunities for faculty and support staff to learn about the strengths and services available to students in an effective middle-level school.
22. *Communications.* There are opportunities for faculty and administrators to communicate the vision statement, the middle-level school concepts, and the desired student outcomes to other educators, administrators, parents, students, and taxpayers.

A matrix of the key indicators of progress that serve as a check sheet while monitoring the transition process is included in Resource E.

Another method of monitoring progress toward an effective middle-level school is to review the findings published in a 1994 study by Keefe, Valentine, Clark, and Irvin, *Leadership in Middle-Level Education,* from the National Association of Secondary School Principals' (NASSP) Commission on School Restructuring. The NASSP study identified 25 middle-level schools that had evidence of success in restructuring (see Table 5.1).

TABLE 5.1 Characteristics of Successful Restructuring

Area of Emphasis	*Characteristics*
Leadership	The leadership team included teachers and principals. Principals enjoyed relative autonomy in personnel and some latitude in budgeting. Parents were active in planning and advising. Leadership was critical in the decision to restructure, good communications, and interdisciplinary teams.
Mission	Mission statements emphasized the needs of young adolescents: support, learning for the future, academic and learning skills, and collaborative processes.
Vision statement	Visions focused on the needs of young adolescents, which were developed in a collegial environment. Visions placed an emphasis on process, supportive school cultures, the leadership of the principal, and staff development.
Vision building	Factors influencing the development of the vision statement were specific practices for involvement; positive school culture; principal leadership; identification of student, parent, and needs; staff development; and defining values and beliefs.
Assumptions and beliefs	Assumptions were based on the need for community involvement, interdisciplinary teaming, high standards, a safe school environment, and adults as role models. Assumptions favored the process of learning and learning to learn rather than content.
Outcomes	Faculty that invested time identifying learning outcomes showed consistency between stated outcomes and actual practices. Faculty with clearly stated learner outcomes tended to use more authentic methods of assessment.

(Continued)

TABLE 5.1 Continued

Process of restructuring	Principals were critical facilitators in vision building, creating support systems, and establishing procedures. Teachers were open to new ideas and comfortable with ongoing change. Teachers participated in decision making about restructuring with principals rather than independently. Typical strategies for restructuring included planning and advisory committees, school improvement teams, interdisciplinary and core teams, group consensus techniques, staff development, and school climate improvement activities.
Middle-level practices	The five essentials to the middle-level schooling model were teaming, exploratory courses, cocurricular programs, advisor-advisee arrangements, and intramural activities.
Middle-level issues and trends	The 6-7-8 grade pattern was most favored in successfully restructured schools. Technology and athletics were similar to other middle or junior high schools. Consistency of beliefs between teachers and principals was significantly higher in the successfully restructured schools. Difficulty associated with change was the same as change at other schools. Students viewed the restructured schools as more friendly than other schools. Students' belief in their ability to succeed was higher in restructured schools than in other schools.
Learning environment	Students and teachers had pride in the physical appearance of their school, which was clean, safe, and orderly. Adult role modeling was emphasized. High academic and behavioral standards were established. Interdisciplinary teams empowered teachers and helped create a sense of ownership. Team organization encouraged openness and risk-taking. There was an emphasis on theme-based curricula and activity-based instruction.

Words of Wisdom

Offering words of wisdom can be difficult because no two schools are the same, and what works in one place may not be effective in another. However, based on some extensive readings and some direct experiences, the following suggestions are presented as a checklist for those undertaking the transition from a junior high school to a middle-level school.

1. *Know the community.* Listening to the desires of the other school administrators and knowing the goals and aspirations of the central office administration, the superintendent, and the school board is essential. Being able to locate allies at all levels, as well as anticipating the questions from special interest groups (the teachers' association, the athletic boosters, the PTA groups, the church groups, etc.) is essential.

Understanding the political implications for groups involved in the transition process is critical. The rational approach to change is often countered by an irrational response. Being prepared for the questions and responding in a comfortable and confident manner may be more important than the substance of what is said to defend the proposal to change a middle school.

2. *Know your faculty and staff.* Taking the faculty and staff for granted will lead to distrust and possible internal sabotage. Special attention should be devoted to scheduled meetings and chance encounters to review the agreed-upon vision and the steps to be taken to reach toward the vision. During the change of routine operations, every ally is important, especially allies that are part of the school.

The group having the strongest credibility in the community is often the support staff (secretaries, custodians, teacher assistants, food service staff, etc.). This group's response to the proposed transition from the junior high school to a middle school is listened to most often because it is perceived as having the least amount of vested interest. This implies that middle-level administrators and faculty may have a stronger influence in explaining the facts about the proposed transition, but the support staff and parents may have a stronger influence on other parents about the less tangible aspects (socialization, exploratory opportunities, core curriculum, advising, etc.) of why the transition to a middle school will be positive for students.

3. *Know about early adolescent behavior.* The philosophy and design of the middle-level grades all centers around the unique needs of early adolescent students. The faculty and support staff should understand and respond to the social, intellectual, emotional, and physical needs of those students.

4. *Know and defend the uniqueness of the middle school.* The major challenge facing middle-level educators is "protecting the uniqueness of the middle-level philosophy." With special interest groups forming coalitions with conservative politicians, there is a substantial network of people who advocate stronger "basic education" with rigor. This same alliance wants to eliminate the school's role in social and emotional development.

At the same time, there is increasing emphasis on measuring teacher accountability by standardized testing. While maintaining the academic performance and rigor that characterizes quality education, middle-level education also places emphasis on other aspects of growth. The middle-level philosophy supports the concept that potential academic ability can be achieved only through the development of all aspects of growth: social, emotional, physical, and intellectual.

Middle-level educators, and especially administrators, need to seek out opportunities to help fellow administrators, school board members, parents, and taxpayers understand the vision. Furthermore, administrators and school board members should address the popularity of "basic" and "rigorous" educational standards in the context of a well-developed philosophy regarding the early adolescent.

5. *Know the reasons why some middle-level school programs are successful.* A review of the research literature will document a wide variety of successful middle-level programs. However, administrators need to understand the researchers' questions, the context of the research, and the potential implications for faculty, students,

and parents. The ability to analyze new findings and ideas implies a need to be an avid reader of relevant journals, attend regional and national professional association meetings, and become actively involved in professional development opportunities. Understanding why a new approach is successful is as important as understanding what it contains.

6. *Know about the uniqueness of your own school.* Your faculty, students, and parents all have different needs and hopes. Your school has some special strengths and some vulnerabilities. Importing a practice that is successful in one school may not be equally successful in another. A critical ingredient to successful change is ownership. The administrator's challenge and opportunity are to provide useful information, trust the participants, and facilitate the decision-making process. Only through the meaningful involvement of those affected by the decision will the transition from a junior high school to a middle-level school be successful.

7. *Know the process and implications of change.* Schools are slow to change, particularly if the change has an impact on different groups in the school. It is slow because people generally do not want to change. Proposing a change in the established order of things is considered a threat to many. Knowing and understanding the implications of a proposed change are very important. People need to be involved and assured about the changes being proposed. There is an old school administrator's axiom that may be appropriate at this point: "There are two primary reasons for being fired. One is to do too much. The other is to do too little. It is your decision."

8. *Know the vision and planning.* If leadership is an episodic event, then management is planning. The planning process is the major activity of the principal. Developing the vision is leadership. Long-range strategic planning is management. How are we going to move toward our vision of what an educational experience should be for early adolescent students? Careful and clear planning of the sequence of events, the involvement of people, the pacing of those events, the use of available resources, and the strategies for recognition are essential. The transition from a junior high school to a middle-level school can take from 3 to 5 years (Clark & Clark, 1989).

9. *Know the payoff for hard work.* A vision of the middle-level school, a focus on the leadership and planning to reach toward that vision, and a self-confident perseverance to withstand the internal and external doubters are crucial contributors to success. The successful transition of a school does not come about by chance, charisma, or coercion. It is the result of effective leadership, careful planning, and hard work.

Conclusion

Making the transition from a junior high school to a middle-level school is a journey. It is leading a community of educators, students, and parents toward an improvement in the education of their children. Because each school has a unique combination of conditions that influences the decision-making process, there is no all-purpose plan or structure that will work for two schools. The transition from a junior high school to a middle-level school requires that a new vision statement and set of strategies for change be developed by the people involved. Usually, because of the complexity of leading and facilitating the day-to-day operations of a school, it is necessary to obtain outside assistance. Planning and facilitating the transition to a middle school cannot be given part-time attention.

An ongoing debate continues about how to balance cognitive learning with the affective needs of the early adolescent; how to group students and to teach and sustain the interest of students, particularly those at risk; the school's role in the development of the core values of trust, loyalty, honesty, and other social responsibilities; and whether the middle-level school reform efforts are a fad or a serious effort to improve schooling. Some school leaders may question the need to change to the middle level when the community is apathetic and complacent about the needs of early adolescent students. Change causes conflict, and the faint at heart may find it wiser to just hold on to what works. The only conciliation when administrators back away from change and conflict is that they may keep their job, but most likely, in the long run, some will find it hard to live with themselves and educational leaders. One of my mentors advised me: "There are generally two ways to leave town. Either you're leading the parade or they are chasing you down Main Street." Again, it is your decision. If proper planning includes the involvement of others, clear communications, and ongoing staff development opportunities, most of the journey will be a rewarding and exciting professional experience.

Resources

RESOURCE A: Characteristics of Unusually Effective Schools: A Planning Guide

Characteristic	Intro-duced	Dis-cussed	Imple-mented
1. Productive school climate and culture			
a. Orderly environment			
b. Faculty commitment to a shared mission			
c. Problem-solving orientation			
d. Faculty cohesion, collaboration, consensus, communications, and collegiality			
e. Faculty input into decision making			
f. Schoolwide emphasis on positive performance			
2. Focus on student acquisition of central learning skills			
a. Maximum availability and use of time for learning			

Characteristic	Intro-duced	Dis-cussed	Imple-mented
b. Emphasis on mastery of central learning skills			
3. Appropriate monitoring of student progress			
4. Practice-oriented staff development at the school site			
5. Outstanding leadership			
a. Vigorous selection and replacement of teachers			
b. Maverick orientation and buffering			
c. Frequent, personal monitoring of school activities			
d. High expenditure of time and energy on improvement			
e. Support for teachers			
f. Acquisition of resources			
g. Superior instructional leadership			
h. Effective use of instructional support personnel			
6. Salient parent involvement			
7. Effective instructional arrangements and implementation			
a. Successful grouping and related arrangements			
b. Appropriate pacing and alignment			
c. Active/enriched learning			
d. Effective teaching practices			
e. Emphasis on higher order learning outcomes			
f. Coordination in curriculum and instruction			

(Continued)

RESOURCE A Continued

Characteristic	Intro-duced	Dis-cussed	Imple-mented
g. Easy availability of abundant materials			
h. Classroom adaptation			
8. High operationalized expectations and requirements			
9. Other possible correlates			
a. Student sense of efficacy/futility			
b. Multicultural instruction and sensitivity			
c. Personal development of students			
d. Rigorous and equitable student promotion policies			

SOURCE: Levine & Lezotte (1990), p. 10.

RESOURCE B: Comparing Middle School to Junior High School Areas of Emphasis

Middle School Emphasis	Junior High School Emphasis
Child-centered program	Subject-centered program
Learning how to learn	Learning a body of knowledge
Comparing with self-potential	Competition with others
Student self-direction, under expert guidance	Adherence to the teacher-made lesson plan
Student responsibility for learning	Teacher responsibility for student learning
Student independence	Teacher control
Flexible (block) scheduling	The six (equal) period day
Variable group sizes	Standard class size
Team teaching	One teacher per class
Self-pacing approach, with students learning at different rates	Textbook approach, with all students on same page at same time

SOURCE: Adapted from information developed by Bondi (1977).

RESOURCE C: Barriers to Change

Barriers to Change	Possible Questions	Strategies
Sense of ownership	What activities will be used to involve others?	
Benefits to those involved	What are the rewards for involvement and support?	
Support for resources (i.e., time and funds)	What are the implications for limited resource? Will resources be taken from other programs?	
Support from above (e.g., district office)	What are the benefits for the superintendent, board, and community?	
Support to others	How will support be given to those involved?	
Security	How will assurances of job security be provided?	
Cultural norms and traditions	How will change affect norms and traditions?	
Order and control	How will the sense of direction be sustained, control balanced, and autonomy preserved?	
Authentic decision making	How will the sense of openness be preserved, and the feeling that there are options?	
Distribution of information	How will the flow of information be equal and accurate?	

(Continued)

RESOURCE C Continued

Barriers to Change	Possible Questions	Strategies
Recognition for involvement	How and when will people be given recognition?	
Pace of change	How will the pace be communicated and monitored?	
Fear of failure	How will the fear of failure be countered? How will negativism be countered?	
Balance of organizational structure	How will balance between system direction and site autonomy be preserved?	

SOURCE: Adapted from Harvey (1990).

RESOURCE D: Vision to Action—Junior High School to Middle-Level School

Vision	Action
Groupings: What are the most effective ways to group students in order to move toward the middle-level vision?	
Emphasis: What criteria does the vision suggest we place more emphasis on and change from our current practices?	
Assumptions: What are the underlying assumptions about future enrollment, community support, and learning theory?	

Vision	Action
Uniqueness: What is the uniqueness and how will these features be presented to attract students and parents?	
Resources: What resources are needed to move toward the vision statement of the middle-level school?	
Plans: What are the plans, timelines, and actions that need to take place to move toward the middle-level vision?	
Results: What overall results can be expected from the transition from a junior high school to a middle school?	
Monitoring: How do we track our progress toward the vision? Are we identifying and resolving those conflicts?	

SOURCE: Adapted from Tregoe et al. (1989). *Vision in Action: Putting a Winning Strategy to Work* (see annotated bibliography).

RESOURCE E: Indicators of Progress Toward Middle-Level Concepts

Indicators of Progress	Questions	Strategies
1. Vision statement	Who owns the vision statement?	
2. Grade alignment	What philosophical base supports the alignment?	
3. Team planning and teaching	How are teachers strengthened and collaboration supported?	

(Continued)

RESOURCE E Continued

Indicators of Progress	Questions	Strategies
4. Interdisciplinary learning	How are teachers planning beyond the core curriculum?	
5. Flexible student grouping	How are students grouped and moved to accommodate different activities?	
6. Flexibility in scheduling	How is the daily schedule designed to meet the needs of students?	
7. Continuous progress	How is flexibility in promotion accommodated to meet student needs?	
8. Individualized instruction	How are independent learning activities arranged?	
9. Instructional materials	How can students use materials designed to meet their interests?	
10. Basic skills	How can students strengthen their basic learning skills?	
11. Exploration	How can students explore a wide variety of interests?	
12. Creative experiences	How can students express creativity in writing, music, art, and drama?	
13. Social development	How can students receive guidance in developing social skills?	

Indicators of Progress	Questions	Strategies
14. Sports activities	How can students learn team spirit and sportsmanship?	
15. Physical development	How can students learn about the physical changes of their bodies?	
16. Individualized guidance	How can students have adult assistance in academic and emotional concerns?	
17. Discussions with adults	How can students have daily interaction with adults?	
18. Social development	How can students learn appropriate values?	
19. Monitoring progress	How do students receive feedback about progress and assistance?	
20. Orientation of new students	How are students assisted in the transition from the self-contained classroom to the departmentalized high school?	
21. Staff development	How can faculty continue to learn and grow?	
22. Communication	How are students, faculty, and parents informed about vision and activities?	

Annotated Bibliography
and References

Annotated Bibliography

Arth, A. A., Bergmann, S. K., Clark, D., Johnston, J. H., Lounsbury, J. H., Toepfer, C. F., Jr., & Melton, G. E. (1989). *Middle level education's responsibility for intellectual development.* Reston, VA: National Association of Secondary School Principals.

This NASSP publication considers the contemporary and emerging issues involved in dealing responsively with young adolescent intellectual development needs. The authors state that the education of young adolescents must be an integrated venture—physical, social, emotional, and intellectual development woven together into the fabric of schooling.

Beane, J. A. (1990). *A middle school curriculum: From rhetoric to reality.* Columbus, OH: National Middle School Association.

This book presents a serious discussion of the middle school curriculum. There is a review of the underlying conception of the whole curriculum at the middle grades. The author claims that the movement toward meeting the needs of young adolescents is not a developmentally appropriate nor responsive approach to the curriculum needs for these students.

Bondi, J. (1977). *Developing middle schools: A guidebook.* Wheeling, IL: Whitehall.

This book is designed for school leaders planning the conversion of a junior high school to a middle school. Emphasis is placed on the characteristics of students, the ideal teacher, the curriculum, possible instructional practices, and a review of various organization structures for successful middle schools.

Carnegie Council on Adolescent Development. (1989). *Turning points: Preparing American youth for the 21st century: The report of the Task Force on Education of Young Adolescents.* Washington, DC: Author.

This report reinforces an emerging movement, still relatively unrecognized by policymakers, to build support for and educate young adolescents through new relationships between schools, families, and health and community institutions. The report contains a comprehensive set of recommendations that is designed to accomplish a fundamental upgrading of education and adolescent development.

Clark, S. N., & Clark, D. C. (1994). *Restructuring the middle-level school: Applications for school leaders.* Albany: State University of New York Press.

The authors have put together a comprehensive review of middle-level education, its historical development, and its present status. They have shown how leaders can implement what is known about developmentally responsive programs for young adolescents. The authors have effectively combined middle school theory and reality with strategies for providing leadership in program implementation.

Crawley, J. (1992). *Constructive conflict management: Managing to make a difference.* San Diego, CA: Pfeiffer & Company.

This book draws on the knowledge and experience of peacekeepers, arbitrators, mediators, and organizational consultants who address one basic question: What are the constructive ways of resolving conflict so that people are able to express and work through differences without the risk of damage to one another? This book targets skills for leaders who are dependent on the contact they have with others, will be more effective if they can become proficient at helping people to get along with each other, and get along with their work.

Educational Research Service. (1983). *Organization of the middle graders: A summary of research.* Arlington, VA: Author.

This research publication addresses the development of both the junior high and middle school movement. Over 180 research studies conducted between 1915 and 1982 are reviewed. Topics include the initiation of the junior high school and middle school; comparisons between the two grade arrangements; effects on emotional, social, and personal development of students; and the attitudes of teachers and administrators toward grade organization. Even in the mid-1990s, this publication is still a valuable source of information about the middle grades.

Epstein, J. L., & Mac Iver, D. J. (1990). *Education in the middle grades: National practices and trends.* Columbus, OH: National Middle School Association.

This publication reports on a comprehensive survey conducted by the Center for Research on Elementary and Middle Schools at Johns Hopkins University involving 2,400 middle grade principals on the degree of implementation of practices that are often recommended for middle grades. It provides a detailed summary of middle-grade trends and practices.

Fenwick, J. J. (1987). *Caught in the middle: Educational reform for young adolescents in California schools.* Sacramento: California State Department of Education.

This book presents the findings and recommendations of the Middle Grades Task Force commissioned by Bill Honig, California State Superintendent of Public Instruction. The book reviews the 22 principles of middle-grade education. Each principle is developed through a discussion of its logic. Included are illustrations, charts, diagrams, excerpts, and catalytic examples for those educators interested in a thorough review of middle-grade reform efforts.

Gruhn, W. T., & Douglass, H. R. (1971). *The modern junior high school* (3rd ed.). New York: John Wiley.

A text designed to provide a comprehensive understanding of the characteristics of the junior high school and middle school. This book provides a review of the historical development of the junior high school and the emerging middle school during the late 1960s and early 1970s.

Hargreaves, A. (1986). *Two cultures of schooling: The case of middle schools.* Philadelphia: Falmer.

Designed to contribute to the debates about the nature and pur-pose of education for children in "the middle years" of school, this book looks at the relationship between two dominant tradi-tions, or cultures, of educational policy and practice on which middle schools have been founded and from which they have grown—the academic-elementary tradition and the develop-mental tradition.

Harvey, T. R. (1990). *Checklist for change: A pragmatic approach to creating and controlling change.* Boston: Allyn & Bacon.

This book is a valuable source of information for those who must facilitate change and those who may be affected by change. It is designed to help leaders learn about creating change more effec-tively and efficiently. The author discusses the strategies that prove useful to people in doing the things they believe ought to be done.

Herman, J. J., & Herman, J. L. (1994). *Making change happen: Practical planning for school leaders.* Thousand Oaks, CA: Corwin.

This book is designed to assist school leaders in understanding and planning change. The authors review a wide variety of planning tools to bring about change in schools. Emphasis is placed on the implications and strategies of long-term strategic planning. The book is organized to serve as a practical reference guide for educators who are responsible and accountable to di-rect change in schools.

Keefe, J. W., Valentine, J., Clark, D. C., & Irvin, J. L. (1994). *Leader-ship in middle-level education, Vol. II: Leadership in successfully restructuring middle schools.* Reston, VA: National Association of Secondary School Principals.

The authors identify 25 middle-level schools that are involved in successful restructuring activities. Leadership and program characteristics of middle-level schools are presented. The last chapter of the book summarizes the most significant findings and offers a composite profile of successfully restructured middle-level schools.

Kouzes, J. M., & Posner, B. Z. (1993). *Credibility: How leaders gain and lose it, why people demand it.* San Francisco: Jossey-Bass.

The authors identify the key to effective leadership: credibility. The findings are based on more than 15,000 people, 400 case studies, and 40 in-depth interviews. Credibility shows how leadership is above all a relationship, with credibility as the cornerstone.

Lawton, D. J. (1989). *A journey through time: A chronology of middle-level education resources.* Columbus, OH: National Middle School Association.

This publication blends both a historical record and contemporary resources related to the middle-grades movement. It is arranged to provide perspective for those involved at the various stages in the transition toward the middle grades.

Levine, D. U., & Lezotte, L. W. (1990). *Unusually effective schools: A review and analysis of research and practice.* Madison, WI: National Center for Effective Schools.

This book is intended to address three continuing questions involving unusually effective schools. First, is the concept of unusually effective schools viable? Second, does the recent research and experience support such a concept? Finally, are the concepts of unusually effective schools compatible with effective district policies and practices? The book contains information about unusually effective schools and processes for creating effective schools.

Lounsbury, J. H. (1991). *Middle school education: As I see it.* Columbus, OH: National Middle School Association.

This book provides an opportunity to review the historical emergence of the middle school movement from the perspective of John Lounsbury, a nationally recognized leader in the reform effort.

Office of Educational Research and Improvement. (1990). *Middle schools in the making: A lesson in restructuring.* Washington, DC: U.S. Department of Education.

This report is not a guide to restructuring the middle school. It is a report of the day-to-day experiences, frustrations, and accomplishments of educators involved in the restructuring process. Stories, concerns, reflections, and recommendations are included in this joint report by the Virginia Education Association and the Appalachia Educational Laboratory.

Riley, P. (1993). *The winner within: A life plan for team players.* New York: Putnam.

This book is about Pat Riley's formula for success. It is about winning, leadership, mastery, change, and personal growth, based on understanding and controlling the shifting dynamics of a team—any team, whether it is a private company or a school. Riley's comments about team building, winning and losing, individuals and cliques, imposed barriers to winning, complacency, and deciding when to move on are very appropriate for school leaders.

Rost, J. C. (1991). *Leadership for the twenty-first century.* New York: Praeger.

An excellent source of scholarly information about leadership for both corporate and school executives. After a careful analysis of previous literature on leadership, the author develops sound definitions of leadership and management. Both definitions provide a fundamental benchmark for the study of administration.

Tregoe, B. B., Zimmerman, J. W., Smith, R. A., & Tobia, P. M. (1989). *Vision in action: Putting a winning strategy to work.* New York: Simon & Schuster.

An excellent source for school administrators who want to learn about the power of a vision. The first half of the book explains how to develop strategies to create a vision statement. The second half deals with implementation. The authors devote a significant amount of effort to the integration of strategy and purpose to organizations and people. Although written for the market and customer orientation, the book is also applicable to education.

Valentine, J. W., Clark, D. C., Irvin, J. L, Keefe, J. W., & Melton, G. (1993). *Leadership in middle-level education, Vol. 1: A national survey of middle-level leaders and schools.* Reston, VA: National Association of Secondary School Principals.

The first of two volumes on the National Study of Leadership in Middle Level Education, this book reports on survey data from a national sample of middle-level principals concerning the personal and professional traits of principals, their job tasks and problems, school programs, and selected educational issues.

Williams, S. C., & Murphy, R. P. (Eds.). (1993). *Developing successful middle schools: Hot topic series.* Bloomington, IN: Center for Evaluation, Development, and Research, Phi Delta Kappa. *This volume offers an insightful look into middle-level education through the eyes of many educators who have fashioned its success and know it best. The book contains 38 journal articles divided into the areas of adolescent needs, middle-level strategies, teaching and curriculum, and leadership. An excellent source of the recent research on middle-level education.*

References

Alexander, W. M., & George, P. S. (1981). *The exemplary middle school.* New York: Holt, Rinehart & Winston.

Beane, J. (1990). Rethinking the middle school curriculum. *Middle School Journal, 21*(5), pp. 1-5.

Bondi, J. (1977). *Developing middle schools: A guidebook.* Wheeling, IL: Whitehall.

Carnegie Council on Adolescent Development. (1989). *Turning points: Preparing American youth for the 21st century: The report of the Task Force on Education of Young Adolescents.* Washington, DC: Author.

Clark, D. C., & Valentine, J. W. (1981). Middle level educational programs: Making the ideal a reality. *NASSP Schools in the Middle,* pp. 1-8.

Clark, S. N., & Clark, D. C. (1989, February). School restructuring: A leadership challenge for middle-level administrators. *NASSP Schools in the Middle,* pp. 1-8.

Commission on the Reorganization of Secondary Education. (1918). *Cardinal principles of secondary education.* Washington, DC: U.S. Department of the Interior, Bureau of Education.

Crawley, J. (1992). *Constructive conflict management: Managing to make a difference.* San Diego, CA: Pfeiffer & Company.

Harvey, T. R. (1990). *Checklist for change: A pragmatic approach to creating and controlling change.* Boston: Allyn & Bacon.

Johnston, J. H., & Markle, G. C. (1983, August). What research says to the practitioner about ability grouping. *Middle School Journal, 14*(4), pp. 28-31.

Kouzes, J. M., & Posner, B. Z. (1987). *The leadership challenge: How to get extraordinary things done in organizations.* San Francisco: Jossey-Bass.

Kouzes, J. M., & Posner, B. Z. (1993). *Credibility: How leaders gain and lose it, why people demand it.* San Francisco: Jossey-Bass.

Levine, D. U., & Lezotte, L. W. (1990). *Unusually effective schools: A review and analysis of research and practice.* Madison, WI: The National Center for Effective Schools.

Lewis, A. C. (1992). Middle schools come of age. *Education Digest, 58*(2), pp. 4-7.

Machiavelli, N. (1952). *The prince* (L. Ricci, Trans.). New York: Oxford University Press.

MacIver, D. J. (1989). *Effective practices and structures for middle grades education.* Charleston, WV: Appalachia Educational Laboratory.

Noar, G. (1961). *Junior high school: Today and tomorrow.* Englewood Cliffs, NJ: Prentice-Hall.

Riley, P. (1993). *The winner within: A life plan for team players.* New York: Putnam.

Rost, J. C. (1991). *Leadership for the twenty-first century.* New York: Praeger.

Toepfer, C. F., Jr. (1988). What to know about young adolescents. *Social Education, 52*(2), 110-112.

Tregoe, B. B., Zimmerman, J. W., Smith, R. A., & Tobia, P. M. (1989). *Vision in action: Putting a winning strategy to work.* New York: Simon & Schuster.